Alyce,
Wealth is 4 All!

"The Financial Truth™" is a Financial Empowerment Book Series.

All rights reserved. No part of this publication may be reproduced, stored in a special system, or transmitted, in any form or by any means, electronic, mechanical, photocopying, recording, or otherwise without prior permission of the publisher.

This publication contains the opinions and ideas of its author and is designed to provide useful advice in regards to the subject matter covered. However, this publication is sold with the understanding that neither the author nor the publisher is engaged in rendering legal, accounting or other professional service. If legal advice or other expert assistance is required, the services of a competent professional person should be sought. The author and publisher specifically disclaim any responsibility for liability, loss or risk, personal or otherwise, that is incurred as a consequence, directly or indirectly, of the use and application of any of the contents of this book.

Notwithstanding anything to the contrary set forth herein, Wealth Builders Publishing House, its officers and employees, affiliates, successors and assignees shall not, directly or indirectly, be liable in any way, to the reader or any other person for any reliance upon the information contained herein, or inaccuracies or errors in or omissions from the book, including but not limited to financial or investment data. Authors warrant that their contributions do not infringe any copyright, violate any property rights, or contain any scandalous, libelous, obscene or unlawful matter or any formula or instruction that may be inaccurate or may be injurious to the user.

"The Road to Wealth Begins with You™" Published by Wealth Builders Publishing House. Copyright 2004-2019 Carla Cargle.
All rights reserved.

14090 Southwest Freeway
Suite 300
Sugar Land, Texas 77478,
(281) 340-2028.

Email: support@carlacargle.com Website: www.carlacargle.com or www.thefinancialtruth.com

Books available for purchase at Wealth Builders Publishing House www.wbphbooks.com.

ISBN-13: 978-0-9768047-0-3

Book Layout & Design: Cristian Rodrguez, Grapho Studios Houston, TX

The Financial Truth™
MISSION STATEMENT

Assist you in building a solid financial foundation.

Help you to develop a spiritual relationship with your money.

Empower you to accumulate wealth and achieve your financial goals.

Building Wealth 4 All

The Financial Truth: The Road to Wealth Begins With You

THE FINANCIAL TRUTH™

Introducing the Newest SuperHero 4

Wealth Builders Money Personality Quiz: Wealth Characteristics 5

Money Personality Quiz: Understanding The Results 7

What is your Money Personality? 9

Letter to Mr. or Ms. "Financial Freedom" Wannabe 12

Session One: The Soul of Your Money 15

What is Wealth? What is Money? 16

Wealth Builders Blueprint 19

Wealth Builders Money Personality Quiz: Financial Stability 22

Blueprint Evaluation 24

Seven Reasons To Track Your Finances 28

What is the financial state of Americans in the 21st century? 32

Guidelines for the Budget Planner and Cash Flow Calculator 33

Budget Planner 34

Cash Flow Calculator..38

Expense Tracker 40

Session Two: Your Wealthy Mindset..........................43

Wealth Builders Money Personality Quiz: Spending Habits............45

Lottery Fact 47

Credit: An Astonishing Fact....................................47

Life's Financial DIPS..49

Five Smart Ways to avoid Ponzi Schemes and Scams..................56

No Savings Plan - No Future Wealth.............................58

Watch Your Savings Grow......................................59

Foundation Repair...60

Net Worth Calculator...62

8 Steps to a Successful Financial Success........................63

9 Ways To Evaluate Your Financial Success.......................65

What's It Worth?..67

Session Three: Your Body's Financial Needs...................69

What is the solution?..70

Develop a Wealthy State of Mind 71

Insurance and Annuity	74
Life Insurance Options	74
Annuity Options	77
And the Question Is...Do You Have Insurance?	78
Life Insurance Calculator	81
Types of Wealth Building Plans	82
Types of Mutual Funds	85
Wealth Building Exercises	87
Wealth Is Relative	89
Wealth Empowerment Oath	90
Conclusion	91
Bio	92
Glossary of Terms	93
Appendix	97
Wealth Builders Money Personality Scoring Guide	98
About the Author	102

I Am T.F. Truth. Let me be your Financial Superhero.

I will teach you how to think wealthy, manage your money, save, and overcome life's financial challenges.

"I Am The Financial Truth. Building Wealth 4 All."

WEALTH BUILDERS MONEY PERSONALITY QUIZ: WEALTH CHARACTERISTICS

Instructions: Please be honest with yourself as you complete this quiz. No one will score the quiz but you. It is strictly confidential. Allow yourself to discover The Financial Truth™ about your money personality.

SD = Strongly disagree D = Disagree
N = Neutral A = Agree
SA = Strongly Agree

1. Driving a luxury car makes feel and look wealthy.

2. The clothes I wear play an important role in my image.

3. Earning a million dollars per year income will make me wealthy.

4. The only way for me to become wealthy is if I win the lottery.

5. Living below my means will help me to become wealthy.

6. I will probably marry into money or inherit my wealth before I accumulate it.

7. Saving for the future is not important to me, I just want to enjoy what I have today.

8. I can become wealthy without investing in real estate, stocks and/or bonds.

9. I need to surround myself with luxury to feel comfortable.

10. Giving to charity is essential to wealth building.

11. I like the security that comes with earning a set paycheck.

12. I consistently save/invest in an account and allow it to accumulate over time.

Count your responses: SD_____ D_____ N_____ A_____ SA_____

To calculate your score, see the Wealth Builders Money Personality Scoring Guide in the Index.

Review the Money Personality Types on pages 7-8.

MONEY PERSONALITY QUIZ: UNDERSTANDING THE RESULTS

Your money personality is a determinant in your ability to build future wealth. It will reveal the habits that have attributed to your financial success or failure. As well, your money personality will help you to identify the areas within your financial mindset that need improvement.

The **"B&B"** money personality is not destined for wealth because of your inability to manage money, control your spending habits, and misinterpretation of what wealth is. Rid yourself of the victim and "welfare" mentality. Therefore if you desire to build wealth, consider patterning your financial behavior like someone whom is **"Balanced"**.

The **"Mattress Mogul"** has the potential to build wealth. However it will probably take two to three times as long to build your wealth than someone who is **"Balanced"**. The **"Mattress Mogul"** does not utilize financial/investment resources and professionals. The growth rate on your "money" will slow up the pace of future wealth. By adding trust to your equation, you can possibly eliminate years from the wealth building process.

"Sales Pro" and **"Livin' Large"** have the financial and mental capacity to become wealthy, but due to your lack of patience and financial wisdom, your chances of becoming wealthy are slim. It is important for you to begin to exercise discipline and self control with your money. Obtaining balance and developing a sound financial plan will be the key to your future wealth.

"Balanced", you live with a solid financial foundation. Life's experiences and your continuous exposure to wealth building principles help you to live according to the "Wealth Builders Blueprint". You have embraced wealth as a holistic state of being.

Continuous financial education and understanding the principles of money management and wealth building is necessary for all the money personalities to successfully build wealth.

"The Road to Wealth begins with You™" will provide you with a basic introduction to the principles of money management, debt management, building a solid financial foundation and wealth building.

It will help you identify the pitfalls that exist within your current "Wealth Builders Blueprint", as well as highlight your financial successes.

What is your Money Personality?

"Mattress Mogul"

You are the type of person who does not want to ever be without money, therefore you do a great job at saving money. However you are more than likely to hoard money, so you won't allow your money to get out of your sight. You will hide money underneath the mattress, shoebox and even bury it in the backyard. You distrust financial institutions and are frugal to a fault.

Tip: Learn to trust others for financial advice. Wealth accumulation requires outside resources.

B&B"

You are "broke and beggin". You have not done a good job at managing your money. As soon as you get a dollar, you spend it. You do not have your money, so whenever you need money you have to beg and borrow from someone else. You are living paycheck to paycheck.

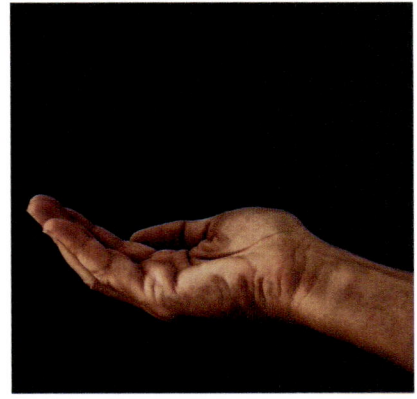

Tip: Become responsible for your own financial situation.

"Sales Pro"

You are a "Professional Shopper". You pay your bills (sometimes), but with every penny left over you spend it at the mall, the dollar store and or the "home shopping channel". Your picture is on display at all of the malls in your area as a "VIP". You are a shopping spree away from going broke.

Tip: Look in your closet/around the house and add up all of the clothes and items with price tags still on them. This is the amount which you could have invested towards your financial freedom.

"Livin' Large"

You are "Livin' Large". You want people to think you have it goin' on. You buy expensive clothes, cars, jewelry, etc. that you cannot afford. You believe that you get more respect because of the "things" that you own. Therefore, you cannot afford the lifestyle that you have created. You are probably deep in debt.

Tip: Learn that wealth is not defined by the "things" that you possess. Stop using your credit cards as a second income.

"Balanced"

You have learned how to live with a balanced budget, a balanced mindset, and a solid financial plan. You have done an excellent job at building a strong financial foundation. You understand that living below your means is essential to building wealth.

Tip: Keep up the good work and share your knowledge and wisdom with others.

Letter to Mr. or Ms. "Financial Freedom" Wannabe

Dear Mr. or Ms. "Financial Freedom" Wannabe,

I have been apart of your life since your allowance or your first job. I usually come to live with you every two weeks.

My purpose is to assist you in creating a stable and comfortable lifestyle, and to help you empower your future.

I'd like to live with you for a very long time.

In fact, I wouldn't at all mind if you added a bunch of others like me to your foundation.

There are certain places that I expect for you to take me. But, because there is a weak level of understanding and communication between us, you don't seem to understand the role I am to play in your life. Therefore, you usually wind up leaving me places where I'll never see you again. Furthermore, you obviously don't know my value, because more often than you should, you exchange me for something that is of lessor value.

I really would like to play a more positive role in your life. It would really be great to see you use me to enrich you and your family's lives. For example, I can help you build wealth and own a piece of the earth.

As well, I'd like for us to be more involved in charity and the community. My constant presence in your life can provide you with a sound peace of mind and the freedom to achieve your dreams.

After helping you live a life of freedom, I'm really looking forward to you introducing me to your grandchildren and or generations to follow.

Sincerely,

Your Money
"The Financial Truth"

Section One:

The Soul of Your Money

Section One addresses the soul of your money. Oftentimes experts have described wealth as strictly a result of making the right investment, owning valuable real estate, signing a large sports contract or receiving a substantial inheritance. True wealth is obtained and sustained through your ability to positively relate to your money and effectively utilize it as a building tool.

WHAT IS WEALTH? WHAT IS MONEY?

In your own words, answer the two questions below:

What is Wealth?

_____
_____
_____
_____

What is Money?

_____
_____
_____
_____

What is Wealth?
What is Money?

Having an abundance of what you need and want.
You are living in the state of Financial freedom.
You are free of "bad" debt.
You are living in a spiritually, mentally and financially sound state of being.
You share your blessings.

A tool not a possession.
Powerless.
Mindless.
Universal language. Asset; measure of wealth.

"The attitude that you give your money determines what your money will do for you and to you."

If your money could talk, what would it say about you and why?

_____

_____

_____

_____

_____

_____

_____

"I'm here to help you not hinder you."

Wealth Builders Blueprint

The Wealth Builders Blueprint is to serve as a model to mold your thought process that will guide you through your wealth journey.

As you study the diagram from bottom to top, you will discover that the soil of your wealth is connected to your soul; what is your money personality? How you think and relate to your money is a reflection of your "spirit" person. Therefore if you dwell in a state of instability, self-doubt, and low self-esteem, then the odds are stacked against you as you strive to live a life of financial freedom. However, if you are focused and determined, strong in faith, and strive to live a balanced life, then your "soul" is fertilized to be able to harvest wealth.

Financial Foundation

The next important aspect of structural design, is laying a strong, solid foundation made of concrete. It is imperative that you have a concrete budget/spending plan, debt management strategy, and cash flow plan in place that acts as the bridge from your "money personality" to your money.

Wealth Pillars

Following laying the foundation, the pillars and beams are put in place to hold the structure together. As you build wealth, risk management more often referred to as insurance, should serve as your pillars to insure that your wealth is sustained in the event of any structural damage (i.e. disability, death, illness, lawsuit, etc.).

Stability and Accumulation

Now that you are building your wealth on "rich soil", a concrete foundation, and the pillars are in place, it is time to incorporate financial stability and wealth accumulation (i.e. savings, real estate, investments, business ownership, annuities, retirement savings, etc.). These are the areas where most people want to begin; yet it is impossible to put on the roof without having the foundation.

Building wealth requires a process and plan. **Utilize the Wealth Builders Blueprint** as your wealth guide. Stay focused and wealth will be in your future.

This is "The Financial Truth".

WEALTH BUILDERS MONEY PERSONALITY QUIZ: FINANCIAL STABILITY

Instructions: Please be honest with yourself as you complete this quiz. No one will score the quiz but you. It is strictly confidential. Allow yourself to discover The Financial Truth about your money personality.

SD = Strongly disagree D = Disagree

N = Neutral A = Agree

SA = Strongly Agree

1. I believe that a sound life insurance plan is important.
2. As long as I pay the minimum credit card payment due, the amount of my credit card debt shouldn't matter.
3. Having a disability income plan is not important to me.
4. An investment plan is more important than an insurance plan.
5. It is better to own a home than to rent.
6. Living with a budget helps me to control my spending.
7. It is acceptable to live at home with my parents to cut down on expenses.
8. I have done a great job managing my money.
9. I find myself getting stressed out over money often.

10. Without adequate health insurance, my financial future could be at risk.

11. When in a relationship, establishing a "family" spending plan is important.

12. Having 3 to 6 months of my monthly expenses in a savings account is essential.

Count your responses: SD_____ D_____ N_____ A_____ SA_____

To calculate your score, see the Wealth Builders Money Personality Scoring Guide in the Appendix.

Review the Money Personality Types on pages 7-8.

BLUEPRINT EVALUATION

Name: _____

Age: _____ Marital Status: _____

Children/Dependents: _____

Occupation: _____ Annual Salary: _____

Money Personality: _____

Do you live according to a household budget? Yes ❑ No ❑

Foundation: (Answer questions based on the amount of coverage you have in force.) (Check one that applies.)

Auto Insurance:
Liability ❑   Comprehensive ❑

Homeowners Insurance:
Yes ❑   No ❑

Health Insurance:
HMO ❑ PPO ❑
Discount Plan ❑ State Assisted ❑
None ❑

Disability Income Insurance:

Work ❑
Personal Policy ❑
Both ❑
None ❑

If you become temporarily or permanently disabled, how much disability income would you receive per month? $ _____

How long would you receive it? _____

Life Insurance:
Work ❏
Personal Policy ❏
Both ❏
None ❏

How much life insurance do you have?
(Do not include Accidental Death.)

$ _____ # of Policies _____

Who are your beneficiaries: _____

Stability
Do you have a checking account? Yes ❏ No ❏
Account Value $ _____

Do you have a savings account? Yes ❏ No ❏
Account Value $ _____

Do you have a money market account: Yes ❏ No ❏
Account Value $ _____

Do you own your own home: Yes ❏ No ❏

Life Insurance Cash Value $ _____

Accumulation:
(List Account values where applicable.)
Retirement Accounts:
IRA $ _____
401k $ _____
403b $ _____
Pension $ _____
Deferred Comp $ _____
Stock: $ _____
Bonds: $ _____
Mutual Funds $ _____
Annuities: $ _____
Education Accounts: $ _____
Business Ownership: $ _____
Real Estate Investments: $ _____
Tax Shelters: $ _____
Speculative Stock Investments: $ _____

Questions: (Circle the number which best describes your feelings.)
How would you describe your current financial situation?

Rate your money management skills. (Budgeting, Debt, etc.)

How do you feel about your financial future?

① ② ③ ④ ⑤

Hopeless → Road to Wealth

Will you ever be wealthy?

① ② ③ ④ ⑤

Not a chance → It's my destiny

Describe the issues that create financial stress in your life:

_____
_____
_____
_____
_____
_____
_____

SEVEN REASONS TO TRACK YOUR FINANCES

Most people work hard to earn their money. Some clock in on a time clock to know the exact amount of hours worked and how much money they have earned. Others keep a mental note of their work hours to measure their salaries validity. Whatever method you use to track your income, you know to the penny if you have been accurately compensated. In fact, if your paycheck or invoice is a dollar short, someone will be held accountable.

Interestingly enough, most people do a great job of tracking their money while they earn it, but a poor job of tracking their money while they spend it. It's as though once money comes into your possession you become possessed. You can't remember where you spend your money, how much money you have spent, and who or what you have spent your money on.

If you really want your hard earned money to positively effect your financial future, here are seven reasons why it is important to track your financial transactions:

| Family |
| Child Care |
| Education |
| Credit Card |
| Car Paym |

1. **Keeps you on target to achieve your goals.**
   Proper planning and effective money management tools, keeps you on target for Financial security;i.e.,adequate savings, debt elimination,insurance planning, home ownership, business ownership, retirement, and wealth accumulation.

2. **Helps you to identify your values.**
   "Where your treasure is, there your heart will be also". Tracking your financial transactions will reveal to you what and who is important in your life. Do you spend more on clothes, shoes, and music, than you do on insurance, investments and education? Do you love your family, but only spend money on yourself?

3. **Maintain control of emotions.**
   Effective communication between you and your money equals little or no financial stress. Less financial stress equals the ability to focus more energy on achieving your goals.

4. **Positive cash Flow.**
   Living below your means enables you to free up money towards saving and investments, charity, and wealth accumulation.

5. **Avoid Financial pitfalls.**
   Overdraft fees, late charges, over the limit fees, high credit card interest rates, and withdrawal penalties are costly and slowly chip into your future wealth. It is best to pay your bills on time, balance your checking account, eliminate high interest credit cards, and avoid early withdrawals from retirement accounts.

6. *Establish a good credit history.*
    Poor Financial habits lead to an unfavorable credit rating. A good credit score provides better access to Financial institutions.

7. *Protect your identity.*
    Identity theft can destroy your Financial integrity. Always be cognizant of who has access to your social security number, credit cards, bank accounts, etc.

WHAT IS THE FINANCIAL STATE OF AMERICANS IN THE 21ST CENTURY?

(U.S. Census 2010) 114,825, 428 million Households

Average Net Worth of Americans by Race and Origin of Households

Race/Origin	Net Worth	Net Worth Excluding Home Equity
African American	$4,955	$1,494
Asian	$69,590	$20,956
Hispanic Origin	$7,424	$3,300
Other	$15,795	$6,391
White	$87,906	$21,810

Average Net Worth per Region

Region	Net Worth	Net Worth Excluding Home Equity
Northeast	$86,758	$17,581
Midwest	$77,769	$21,871
South	$57,079	$11,002
West	$57,034	$16,503

Footnote: Regardless of where you are represented in the statistical data reported, Americans must do a better job in building wealth.

GUIDELINES FOR THE BUDGET PLANNER AND CASH FLOW CALCULATOR

Within Corporate America, small businesses, religious institutions, and community based organizations, you are required to live according to their financial guidelines to achieve what each defines as financial success. You readily work within their budget constraints and assist them in documenting their expenses. You accept a 3% raise from your employer because that is all that the budget will allow. You will keep an accurate record of your expenses for your company's profit and loss statement.

How interesting it is, that you efficiently apply money management principles within the workplace and community, but abandon these practices at home.

It is time to make your personal financial success a priority.

Incorporate the following financial tools within your wealth building practices.

→ 1 Budget Planner
→ 2 Cash Flow Calculator

The Budget Planner helps you to stay focused on your spending goals (i.e. Household Savings/Investments, Taxes, Debt, Charity, etc.) Create an Ideal Model Budget for your family. And with the help of the Cash Flow Calculator, periodically compare your actual spending to your Ideal Model Budget. Incorporating these financial tools within your wealth building process should help you stay on target as you build wealth.

The Financial Truth® Budget Planner

	PROJECTED MONTHLY AMOUNT	ACTUAL MONTHLY AMOUNT	DIFFERENCE
Gross Income	$ _____	_____	_____
Pre-tax contributions	- _____	_____	_____
Taxable Income	= _____	_____	_____

TAXES/EMPLOYEE BENEFITS

Federal	$ _____	_____	_____
Social Security	+ _____	_____	_____
Employee Benefits	+ _____	_____	_____
Total Taxes/Employee Benefits	= _____	_____	_____

Taxable Income	$ _____	_____	_____
Total Taxes/Employee Benefits	- _____	_____	_____
After Tax/Benefit Income	= _____	_____	_____

CHARITABLE GIFTS (10%)*

Religious Contributions	$ _____	_____	_____
Other Charities	+ _____	_____	_____
Total Charitable Gifts	= _____	_____	_____

SAVINGS/INVESTMENTS (10%)*

Emergency Savings	$ _____	_____	_____
Educational Fund	+ _____	_____	_____
Individual Retirement Acct.	+ _____	_____	_____
Investment Account	+ _____	_____	_____
Total Savings/Investments	= _____	_____	_____

| | PROJECTED MONTHLY AMOUNT | ACTUAL MONTHLY AMOUNT | DIFFERENCE |

HOUSEHOLD EXPENSES (30%)*

Rent/Mortgage	$ _____	_____	_____
Utilities	+ _____	_____	_____
Groceries	+ _____	_____	_____
Lawn/Alarm	+ _____	_____	_____
Furniture	+ _____	_____	_____
Total Household Expenses	= _____	_____	_____

RISK MANAGEMENT (5%)*

Health Insurance	$ _____	_____	_____
Personal Life Insurance	+ _____	_____	_____
Disability Insurance	+ _____	_____	_____
Dental/Vision Insurance	+ _____	_____	_____
Auto Insurance	+ _____	_____	_____
Renter's Insurance	+ _____	_____	_____
Doctor's Visits	+ _____	_____	_____
Total Risk Management (other than benefits)	= _____	_____	_____

DEPENDENT CARE EXPENSES (10%)*

Children: Day Care, Etc.	$ _____	_____	_____
Household Pet	+ _____	_____	_____
Total Dependent Care Expense	= _____	_____	_____

TRANSPORTATION EXPENSES (12%)*

Car Note	$ _____	_____	_____
Gas	+ _____	_____	_____
Repairs/Maintenance	+ _____	_____	_____
Parking/Tolls	+ _____	_____	_____
Inspection/Emission	+ _____	_____	_____
Total Transportation Expenses	= _____	_____	_____

	PROJECTED MONTHLY AMOUNT	ACTUAL MONTHLY AMOUNT	DIFFERENCE

INSTALLMENT DEBT (10%)*

Credit Cards	$ _____	_____	_____
Loans	+ _____	_____	_____
Total Installment Debt	= _____	_____	_____

ENTERTAINMENT/TRAVEL (5%)*

Dining Out	$ _____	_____	_____
Movies	+ _____	_____	_____
Social/Clubs	+ _____	_____	_____
Music/CD/Streaming Services	+ _____	_____	_____
Travel/Vacation	+ _____	_____	_____
Total Entertainment/Travel	= _____	_____	_____

PERSONAL CARE (5%)*

Laundry	$ _____	_____	_____
Grooming	+ _____	_____	_____
Clothing	+ _____	_____	_____
Total Personal Care	= _____	_____	_____

MISCELLANEOUS EXPENSES (3%)*

Cell Phone/Pager	$ _____	_____	_____
Cable	+ _____	_____	_____
Professional Fees	+ _____	_____	_____
Periodicals	+ _____	_____	_____
Total Miscellaneous Expenses	= _____	_____	_____

GRAND TOTAL

Charity, Savings, Expenses = _____ _____ _____

The Financial Truth® Cash Flow Calculator

MONTHLY AMOUNT

Gross Income $ _____

Pretax Contributions − _____

Taxable Income = _____

TAXES/EMPLOYEE BENEFITS

Federal $ _____

Social Security + _____

Employee Benefits + _____

Total Taxes
Employee Benefits = _____

Taxable Income $ _____

Total Taxes
Employee Benefits − _____

**After Tax
Benefit Income** = _____
(taxable income - total taxes /employee benefits)

CHARITABLE GIFTS (10%)*

Religious Contributions $ _____

Charitable Donations + _____

Gifts Family/Friends + _____

Total Charitable Gifts = _____

SAVINGS/INVESTMENTS (10%)*

MONTHLY AMOUNT

Emergency Savings $ _____

Educational Fund + _____

Individual
Retirement Account + _____

Investment Account + _____

**Total Savings
Investments** $ _____

DEPENDENT CARE EXPENSES (10%)*

Children: Day Care, etc $ _____

Household Pet + _____

**Total Dependent
Care Expense** = _____

TRANSPORTATION EXPENSES (12%)*

Car Note $ _____

Gas + _____

Repairs/Maintenance + _____

Parking/Tolls + _____

Inspection/Emission + _____

Total Transportation Expenses = _____

INSTALLMENT DEBT (10%)*

Credit Cards $ _____

Loans + _____

Total Installment Debt = _____

ENTERTAINMENT/TRAVEL (5%)*

MONTHLY AMOUNT

Dining Out	$_____
Movies	+_____
Social/Clubs	+_____
Music/CD	+_____
Travel/Vacation	+_____
Total Entertainment/Travel	=_____

HOUSEHOLD EXPENSES (30%)*

Rent/Mortgage	$_____
Utilities	+_____
Groceries	+_____
Lawn/Alarm	+_____
Furniture	+_____
Total Household Expenses	=_____

RISK MANAGEMENT (5%)*
Other than empl. benefits

Health Insurance	$_____
Personal Life Insurance	+_____
Disability Insurance	+_____
Dental/Vision Insurance	+_____
Auto Insurance	+_____
Renter's Insurance	+_____
Doctor's Visits	+_____
Total Risk Management	=_____

PERSONAL CARE (5%)*

MONTHLY AMOUNT

Laundry	$_____
Grooming	+_____
Clothing	+_____
Total Personal Care	=_____

*(MISCELLANEOUS EXPENSES (3%)

Cell Phone/Pager	$_____
Cable	+_____
Professional Fees	+_____
Periodicals	+_____
Total Miscellaneous Expenses	=_____

GRAND TOTAL MONTHLY EXPENDITURES

Charity, Savings, Expenses	=_____
After Tax/Benefit Income	$_____
minus	
Grand Total Expenses	-_____
Positive/ (Negative) Cash Flow	=_____

The Financial Truth® Expense Tracker

Utilize the Expense Tracker daily to assist you
in maintaining your Budget

WHERE?	ON WHAT?	HOW MUCH ($)	WHY?	CASH/CREDIT	BUDGET: Y/N	NEED/WANT

WHERE?	ON WHAT?	HOW MUCH ($)	WHY?	CASH/CREDIT	BUDGET: Y/N	NEED/WANT

42

Section Two:

Life's Financial D.I.P.S.

Section Two focuses on converting your inner thoughts about money to mental choices shown through your money management skills, i.e. credit, debt management, savings, etc.

Building wealth and creating "consumptive" debt are not synonymous. In other words, it is counterproductive to build a house and tear it down at the same time.

As you receive "The Financial Truth" and follow the wealth blueprint, it is important to make the choice to become an accumulator of appreciable assets and stop living as a consumer of depreciable assets.

However, if you currently find yourself in the position where you have created an overwhelming amount of debt, this section should assist you in surfacing from debtor's hell.

The choice is yours to live a life of Financial bondage or Financial freedom.

WEALTH BUILDERS MONEY PERSONALITY QUIZ: SPENDING HABITS

Instructions: Please be honest with yourself as you complete this quiz. No one will score the quiz but you. It is strictly confidential. Allow yourself to discover The Financial Truth about your money personality.

SD = Strongly disagree

D = Disagree

N = Neutral

A = Agree

SA = Strongly Agree

1. I can "window shop" without spending any money.
2. Shopping helps me to relieve stress.
3. I will only live once, therefore charge "it" to the maximum.
4. I will stop at nothing to get the things that I want.
5. If I'm ever unable to manage my debt, filing bankruptcy will be a viable option.
6. I prefer to pay cash for smaller ticket items. ($100.00 or less)
7. I prefer to shop at thrift stores, consignment stores and wholesale/discount stores.

8. I usually pay my bills with money orders.

9. I purchase items when they are on sale, even if I don't need them.

10. I often use a Pay Day Advance business to help me make it to my next check.

11. Keeping a "large" stash of cash in my house helps me to feel secure.

12. When I spend money I feel powerful.

Count your responses: SD_____ D_____ N_____ A_____ SA_____

To calculate your score, see the Wealth Builders Money Personality Scoring Guide in the Appendix, or take the personality quiz online for instant results.

Review the Money Personality Types on pages 7-8.

LOTTERY FACT

In the year 2010, Americans spent 50 billion dollars on the lottery. 32.8 billion was returned in prize money. In 2011, there was $63 billion dollars in sales in the lottery, with a net profit of $18.4 billion.

CREDIT: AN ASTONISHING FACT

By the year 2012, Americans had managed to create over $11,000,000,000,000 (11 trillion) dollars of outstanding debt.

$11.38 Trillion in total debt

$8.52 billion credit card debt
$8.15 trillion mortgage debt
$9.14 billion student debt

There are 1.8 billion credit cards circulating within the United States. From 10/2005 - 09/2017 about 12.8 million consumer bankruptcy petitions were filed. (Source: U.S. Courts)

40% of families in the United States spend more money than they earn each year. How?

Credit Cards.
How much credit should you have?

Credit Card
Visa, American Express, MasterCard, Discover = Universal Acceptance

Store Card
Macy's, Sears, Texaco, etc. = *Accepted only by the specific retailer*

It is not necessary to have store cards and credit cards. One to two credit cards are needed with a credit limit of no more than $3000 to $5000. Credit cards should not be used as a source of part time income.

Life's Financial DIPS.

How to manage Debt, navigate through Identity Theft, and avoid Ponzi Schemes.

(Debt, Identity Theft, and Ponzi Schemes)

Debt

To many, debt is a necessity to meet life's needs and wants. Credit cards, student loans, car loans, mortgage loans, payday loans; all are forms of debt and sometimes referred to as OPM. (Other People's Money.) It is often encouraged to use OPM when making a major purchase; (house, car, boat, student loan, etc.) However, it should be used in moderation. What often happens is you become dependent on OPM and abandon MOM, (My Own Money) and then your debt becomes unmanageable.

Personal Finance and the Credit Card

Many believe that it is en vogue to have a portfolio of credit cards. After all, the more credit cards a person has, the more money they must earn, right? And let's not forget about the color of your credit card. How prestigious it must be to pull a platinum or black American Express, VISA, MasterCard, and / or Discover out of your wallet; right? For the sake of clarity let me point out to you what your credit card does not represent:

1. Status Symbol. Don't define who you are financially by the color of your credit card(s). How much credit you have been extended is not a measure of your net worth. In fact, the less money that goes toward paying credit card bills every month, the more money you have available for building your future wealth. Credit Tip: You only need one to two major credit cards.

2. Your Second Income. Your approach to credit might be, the more credit I have, the more money I can spend. With credit I can buy all the things I am unable to afford with my income. Credit Tip: An individual generally only needs up to $5000 credit limit.

3. Free Money. When you convert the credit that has been extended to you to debt, it is your responsibility to pay it back. Credit Tip: Don't use your credit cards with the thought that if I'm unable to pay, I will file bankruptcy.

When credit is used wisely, it can enhance your financial integrity. When you buy a house, car, open a bank account, etc. your credit report is reviewed to determine your ability to manage credit. It measures if you have paid your bills on time and how many years you have managed credit. As well, some employers review your credit report to determine your level of financial trustworthiness. The following are three ways to use credit to your advantage.

1. Make timely payments. Timely payments reflect positively on your credit report.

2. Great record keeping. The statement assists in evaluating your spending. This capability is most advantageous as you maintain your cash flow calculator and budget planner.

3. Financial Leverage. In addition to having an emergency savings account, having available credit, (credit cards, line of credit) gives you a sense of security.

Beware!!! Bad Debt Alert!
Pay Day Loans

You get in a financial crunch and tell yourself that you just need a little help until payday. So rather than borrow money from a friend, you visit your friendly Pay Day Loan establishment. According to the Center for Responsible Lending, "A pay day loan is typically for a few hundred dollars, with a term of two weeks, and an interest rate as high as 800 percent. The average borrower ends up paying back $793 for a $325 loan." The exorbitant fees can make it difficult to maintain your budget. If you were unable to manage your finances before the pay day loan, the ridiculously high interest rate and payback amount could adversely affect your financial stability and lead to bankruptcy.

> **THOUGHT BOX**
>
> Wise advice regarding Pay Day Loans – Don't Do It!!!

Identity Theft

Identity Theft can be emotionally and financially devastating to an individual's credit history and financial stability The Identity Theft and Assumption Deterrence Act of 1998 says that identity theft is when someone "knowingly transfers or uses, without lawful authority, a means of identification of another person with the intent to commit, or aid or abet, any unlawful activity that constitutes a violation of Federal law, or that constitutes a felony under any applicable State or Local law."

Criminals perpetrate identity theft through the Internet, ATM machines, and gas pumps by obtaining access to your confidential financial data through your transaction history. As well they have other tricks up their sleeves such as:

Shoulder surfing — where someone looks over your shoulder while you are conducting personal financial business. Solution: Be mindful of people in your private space.

Prey on your carelessness — if you lose your wallet or purse this provides them with open access to your information. Solution: Keep your social security card at home in a safe secure place.

Treasure Trash — they hunt through your trash searching for discarded credit card statements, bank statements, etc. Solution: Shred old financial records and confidential information.

Intercept your mail looking for pre-approval letters from credit card companies. Solution: — you can opt out of receiving some of the per-approval letters by contacting (888) 5-OPTOUT (888- 567-8688).

Other ways to avoid Identity Theft:

1. Never provide your social security number on an unsolicited phone call.

2. When it is necessary for you to confirm your identity, only provide the last four digits of your social security #.

3. Subscribe to a credit monitoring service.

4. Collect your mail every day from your mailbox.

5. Setup password access to your cell phone. This prohibits others from accessing confidential data on your cell phone.

6. Avoid accessing personal and confidential information on unsecured Wi-Fi; public restaurants, hotels, etc.

7. Setup bank alerts and credit card alerts on your cell phone and / or email. This will keep you abreast of your balance, withdrawals, charges, etc.

The major credit reporting agencies and most banks provide an identity theft tracking service. You pay them a set amount every month and they notify you when there is activity on your credit report.

Major Credit Reporting Agencies:

Equifax P.O. Box 105788 Atlanta, GA 30348 (888) 548 ‚Äì 7878 www.equifax.com

Trans Union P.O. Box 390 Springfield, PA 19064-0390 (800) 916 ‚Äì 8800 www.transunion.com

Experian P.O. Box 2104 Allen, TX 75013-2104 (888) 397-3742 www.experian.com

Internet websites to obtain an instant copy of your credit report for free:

www.annualcreditreport.com
www.creditkarma.com
www.creditsesame.com
www.truecredit.com

You are entitled to receive a free copy of your credit report once per year from each major credit bureau. As well, if you have been denied credit, you can obtain a copy of your credit report from the main credit reporting agency which provided the information to the company which denied you credit.

Scams and Ponzi Schemes

"Ponzi" schemes promise high financial returns or dividends not available through traditional investments. Instead of investing the funds of victims, however, the con artist pays "dividends" to initial investors using the funds of subsequent investors (FBI.gov).
Visit the FBI website for a complete list of common frauds and schemes.
www.fbi.gov/scams-and-safety/common-fraud-schemes.

The spirits of *Never Enough* and *Not Enough* make one susceptible to Ponzi schemes and scams that prey on the *Need More* mentality. It is my belief that greed and poverty are twins born from the same state of consciousness and inspired by the same type of emotion. Both states of consciousness perpetuate the never enough / not enough mentality. Greed (never enough) and Poverty (not enough) = *Need More*. If you are looking for the big score or want something for nothing than you are a prime target for a Ponzi scheme. Avoid double digit guaranteed interest rates and high monthly income distribution rates. Be satisfied and grateful for what you have. The universe will always give a grateful heart something more to be grateful for.

Additionally, perpetrators of Ponzi schemes and scams are often described to have the Halo effect. Some render themselves to the public as religious leaders and / or influential business leaders with angelic and trustworthy reputations. The victim is blinded by the light, abandons common sense and falls prey to the fraud.

Five Smart Ways to avoid Ponzi Schemes and Scams

1. **Confirm the person has a license to promote the investment.**
   Visit their website and click on the FINRA Broker Check link. All credible Financial Advisors will have a FINRA regulated website. And are required to have a link to FINRA to provide the public access to their record.

2. **Don't believe that you are special because no one else you know has the 18% guaranteed rate that you've been promised.**
   If it is too good to be true, it's because it is not true!

3. **Setup online access to your account.**
   Most scammers only provide false paper account statements. If they don't provide you with on-line access to your account information, it's because there is no account information.

4. **Know who is managing your money.**
   Financial Advisors earn a respectable living; however, most are not earning Bentley and Multi-Million Dollar Mega Mansion money. I'm not saying it is not possible, though it is not probable based on the median Advisor's income. If there is too much Bling, it's a chance they're on the way to Sing Sing.

5. **Know the Investment.**
   Private investments such as precious metals exploration, foreign securities, dinosaur breeding; perform due diligence before you invest. Do your money a favor, research it; if you Google it, you might not lose it.

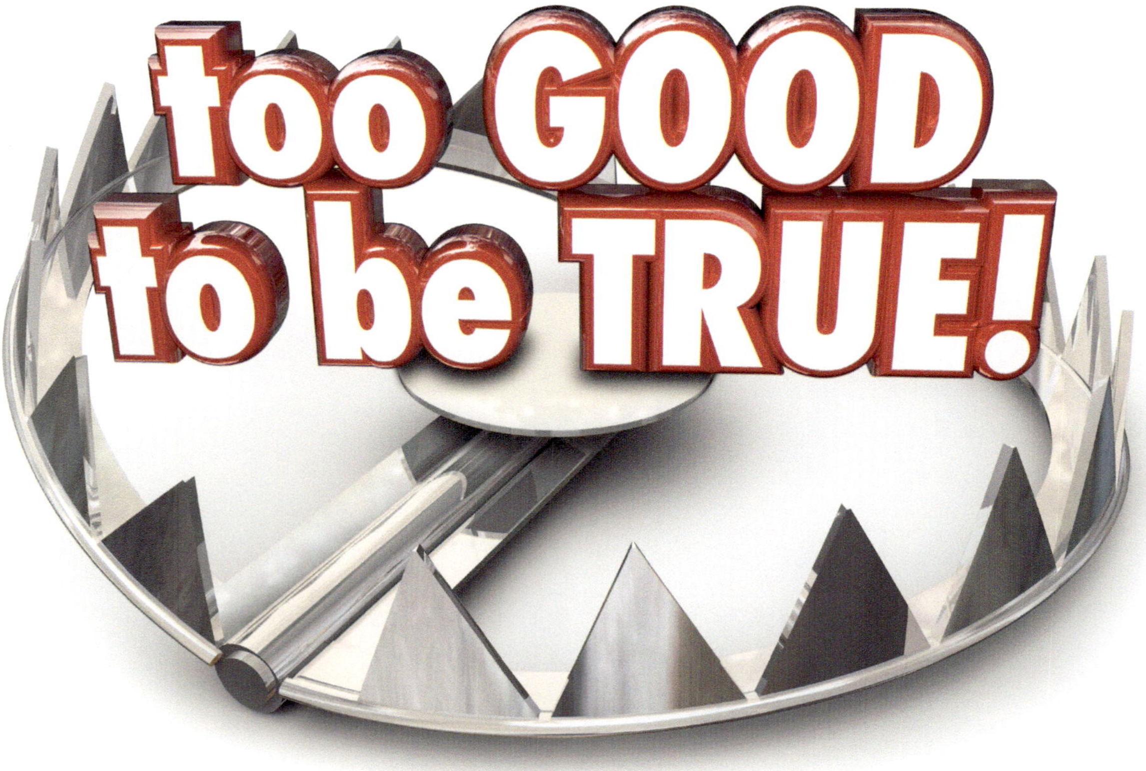
too GOOD
to be TRUE!

NO SAVINGS PLAN - NO FUTURE WEALTH

Reasons Why People Don't Save

"I'll start saving money when I get out of debt."
"I don't make enough money to save."
"I don't trust the bank."
"I don't know where to save my money."
"It's hard to save money once I get it in my hands."

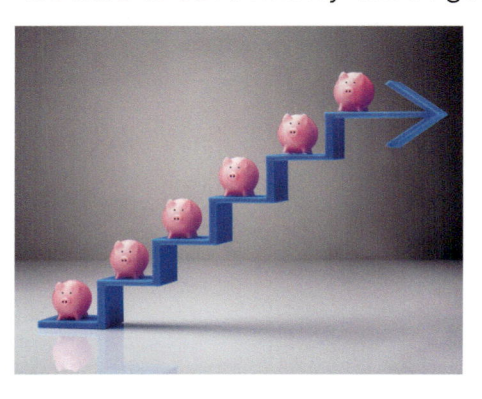

Developing a Savings Plan

Credit Union Account

Money Market Account

Regular Savings through your bank

Begin savings with a realistic amount:

→ Minimum $25.00 per month

→ It is best to have your savings deducted from your paycheck (If you don't touch it, you can't spend it.)

Time + Consistent Savings = Road to Wealth

Consult with a trusted licensed financial professional to develop a financial plan.

WATCH YOUR SAVINGS GROW

Savings Assumptions
$50.00 per month = $600.00 per year
Number of Years to Save = 20 years
Marginal Tax Rate = 15%
Annual Increase to Savings = 10% per year
Pretax Return on Savings = 6.00%

Year	Annual Savings + Increase 10%	Beginning Balance	Interest 6.00%	Taxes 15.00%	Ending Balance
1	$600	$600	$36	$5	**$631**
2	660	1291	77	12	**1356**
3	726	2082	125	19	**2189**
4	799	2987	179	27	**3140**
5	878	4018	241	36	**4223**
6	966	5189	311	47	**5454**
7	1063	6517	391	59	**6849**
8	1169	8018	481	72	**8427**
9	1286	9714	583	87	**10209**
10	1415	11624	697	105	**12216**
11	1556	13773	826	124	**14475**
12	1712	16187	971	146	**17013**
13	1883	18896	1134	170	**19859**
14	2071	21931	1316	197	**23049**
15	2278	25328	1520	228	**26619**
16	2506	29126	1748	262	**30611**
17	2757	33368	2002	300	**35070**
18	3033	38103	2286	343	**40046**
19	336	43382	2603	390	**45594**
20	3670	49264	2956	443	**51776**

FOUNDATION REPAIR

Identify financial/spending habits, which create cracks in your financial foundation. Try to create a list of at least 10.

_____
_____
_____
_____
_____
_____

Now that you have identified these habits, tell them one by one

The Financial Truth™

"You are the weakest link, Bye bye"

61

NET WORTH CALCULATOR

To determine your net worth, calculate your assets (monetary value) and your liabilities (balance due). The difference between your total assets and your total liabilities is your Personal Net Worth.

Asset	Monetary Value

CURRENT LIQUID ASSETS
Checking Account _____
Savings Account _____
Credit Union Account _____
Money Market Account _____
Certificate of Deposit _____
Treasury Note _____
U.S. Savings Bonds _____
Sub-total Current Assets _____

LONG-TERM ASSETS
Insurance (cash value) _____
Annuities _____
IRA, 401K, 403b _____
Profit Sharing Plans _____
Pension Fund _____
Business Interest _____
Sub-total Long-Term Assets _____

PERSONAL PROPERTY
Clothing, Furs, etc. _____
Automobiles _____
Jewelry _____
Furniture & Fixtures _____
Other _____
Sub-total Personal Property _____
Total Assets _____

Asset	Monetary Value

INVESTMENTS
Personal Residence _____
Rental Property _____
Mutual Funds _____
Stocks, Bonds, Commodities _____
Fine Art _____
Other _____
Sub-total Investments _____

Liabilities	Balance Due

CURRENT LIABILITIES
Current Bills _____
(Due in 60 days or less) _____
Sub-total Current Debt _____

REAL ESTATE
Mortgage _____
Rental Property _____
Other Real Estate _____
Sub-total Real Estate Debt _____

INSTALLMENT DEBT
Automobile Loan _____
School Loan _____
Bank Loan _____
Credit Cards _____
Sub-total Installment Debt _____
Total Liabilities _____

Personal Net Worth _____ (Totals Assets - Total Liabilities)

8 STEPS TO A SUCCESSFUL FINANCIAL FUTURE

1. *Relate positively with your money.*
   Positivity plays a major role in your financial success. You must have a positive cash flow, a positive net worth, positive account balances, positive investment returns, positive relationships, and a positive attitude.

2. *Solid insurance plan.*
   There is nothing glamorous about insurance, but it is the foundation of a sound financial plan. Insurance is another form of money. As you build your wealth, insurance serves as the security blanket that helps you sustain your financial assets.

3. *Maintain an adequate savings plan.*
   The rule of thumb is to maintain at least 3 to 6 months of your net monthly expenses in a money market savings account. This account supports you when emergencies occur., i.e. job transition, disability, family emergency, etc. Guaranteed account balance and immediate liquidity are more important than the rate of return.

4. *Sound investment portfolio.*
   A successful investment strategy is diversified with stocks, bonds, mutual funds and/or annuities. In order to reduce your tax consequences during the accumulation period, structure your investments in tax-advantaged accounts. As well, "The Millionaires Next Door" (Authors: Danko/Stanley) created their wealth with the help of a consistent and disciplined plan. Utilize the Dollar Cost Averaging method for better growth potential.

5. **Invest in Real Estate.**
   Real estate is a sound investment. As rental property, it can provide a steady flow of income. Every person who has ever obtained financial freedom owns real estate. Real estate does not provide for immediate liquidity, therefore it is not wise to have all of your net worth linked to real estate.

6. **Continuous Financial Education.**
   Knowledge is power. Achieving financial success requires that you read financial literature, attend seminars and workshops, stay abreast of new opportunities, associate with like-minded people, and find a mentor who has achieved the success that you are striving for.

7. **Share your wealth.**
   One aspect of financial success is the ability to see your money positively impacting your family and community. If you only want to create wealth for your own selfish desires, there is no honor or success in that. Giving is an important component to receiving.

8. **Have an exit strategy.**
   Since life is uncertain, it is important to insure that the assets that you have accumulated throughout your life will not vanish overnight. Appoint an executor/executrix over your estate. Seek legal counsel to prepare a valid will and trusts, when applicable. Leave your assets with someone who is responsible and will value your legacy.

9 WAYS TO EVALUATE YOUR FINANCIAL SUCCESS

Achieving financial success is something that you subconsciously desire. You have played the lottery at least once, praying that you would win. Or you have played along on "Who Wants to Be a Millionaire", wishing you had a chance at the million dollars. Maybe, you are just striving to become debt-free and have money left over after your bills are paid. However you define financial success, here are nine ways to evaluate if you are on target to achieve it.

1. **Outstanding debt has decreased.**
   A reduction in your outstanding debt represents an increase in your positive cash flow.

2. **Financial account values have increased.**
   Savings accounts, investment accounts, retirement accounts, etc. have increased in value therefore you are moving forward in a positive direction towards wealth accumulation.

3. **No more financial transaction penalties.**
   You are practicing efficient money management techniques because you are no longer paying overdraft charges, over the limit fees, and/or late fees.

4. **No longer a Shopaholic.**
   Your picture is no longer posted in the "VIP" section in your neighborhood mall. You have learned that your financial freedom is not associated with your wardrobe or "things" you buy.

5. *Appreciable assets exceed Depreciable assets.*
   You understand that as you spend your money it eventually should flow back to you with an increased worth.

6. *You have a positive cash flow.*
   You are no longer living paycheck to paycheck. You are not operating in a deficit. You are depositing your excess funds in your savings and/or investment plan. You are living below your means.

7. *Financial peace of mind.*
   You no longer worry about your financial future because you have developed successful financial habits. Arguments with your spouse, significant other, or yourself regarding money have diminished.

8. *Net Worth = 10% Rule.*
   The rule of thumb is to save 10% of your income per year. Add up what you have earned since you have entered the full time workforce multiply it by 10%. Your net worth should at least be equivalent to 10% of your accumulated earnings.
   Example: Average salary $35,000 per year. # of years in the workforce = 12
   $35,000 @12 = $420,000 @ 10% = net worth should at least be $42,000 (Net Worth = Assets minus liabilities + owner's equity)

9. *Accomplishing Goals on Priority List.*
   A written plan with goals and a timeline is needed to keep you on pace to achieve financial success. Concentrate on one goal at a time. Accomplishing one task is better than failing at two.

WHAT'S IT WORTH?

Is it an appreciable (A), or depreciable asset (D)? What do you own?

Coach Bag _____

Michael Jordan Baseball Card _____

CLK Mercedes Benz 2005 _____

Real Estate _____

Gucci Suit _____

Apple Stock _____

A pair of Jimmy Choo Shoes _____

Diamond Jewelry _____

Neiman Marcus Gift Card _____

Retirement Account _____

Xbox _____

529 Plan _____

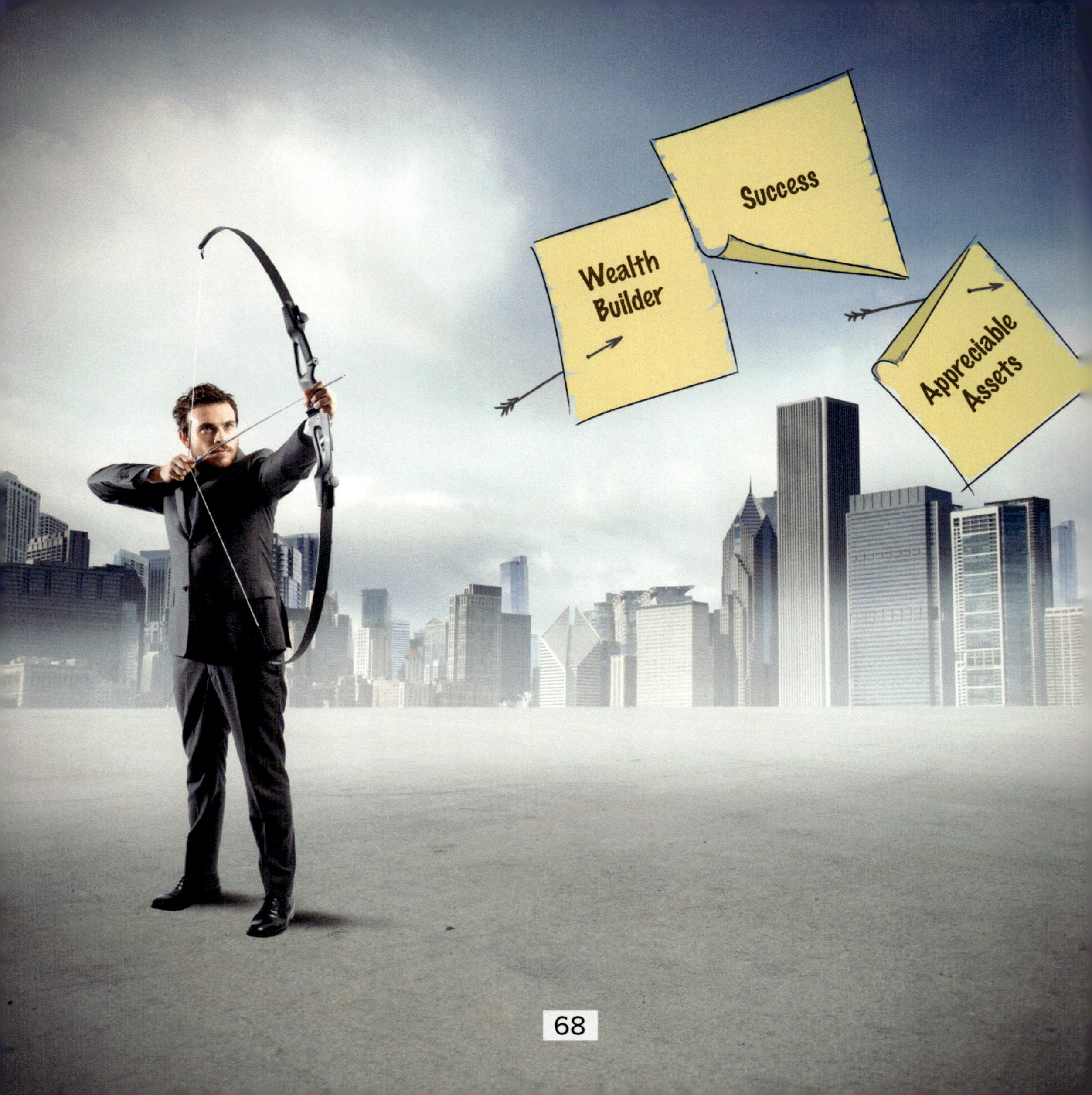
Success
Wealth Builder
Appreciable Assets

Section Three:

Your Body's Financial Needs

Section Three touches the surface of how you nurture your body's financial needs. It introduces you to the financial tools that will secure and build your wealth.

WHAT IS THE SOLUTION?

Develop a "Wealthy State of Mind"

Depreciable Assets to Appreciable Assets
- Depreciable assets decrease in value
- Appreciable assets increase in value

Consumption Plan to Accumulation Plan
Consumption plan = spends money
Accumulation Plan = save/invest money

Wealth Destroyer to Wealth Builder

Wealth Builder - Characteristics and Ownership
- Characteristics
- Disciplined
- Active plan and budget
- Seek knowledge
- Holistic
- Positive

Aim for financial success
Ownership
- Real Estate
- Stocks and Bonds
- Mutual Funds
- Life Insurance & Annuity
- Business Ownership

DEVELOP A WEALTHY STATE OF MIND

*"Wealth must manifest itself within your mind
before it can exist in the tangible."*

The world is fixated on "The Lifestyles of the Rich & Famous" and the homes of celebrities on "Cribs". So many people want to be "rich, live large, roll in the dough, drive a Bentley, and wear the bling, bling". However, if you really want to admire the "wealthy", admire them for their mindset, not their money.

The money and assets are a byproduct of their mindset. Before the financial assets were attained, their mind endured a rigorous test. Goals were set, plans were developed, and sacrifices were made. The wealthy make well thought out decisions and wise choices with their finances. They are interested in accumulation, not consumption. They understand the difference between appreciable assets vs. depreciable assets. The affluent have mastered the flow of money. As they release their money into the flow of the economy, it returns back to them in the form of capital gains, dividends, real estate, business ownership, etc. In addition, the wealthy understand that "as a person thinketh, so is he/she". Therefore they speak positively about their money. Negative thoughts are not allowed to exist in their mindset.

Are your thoughts destroying your opportunity for financial freedom?

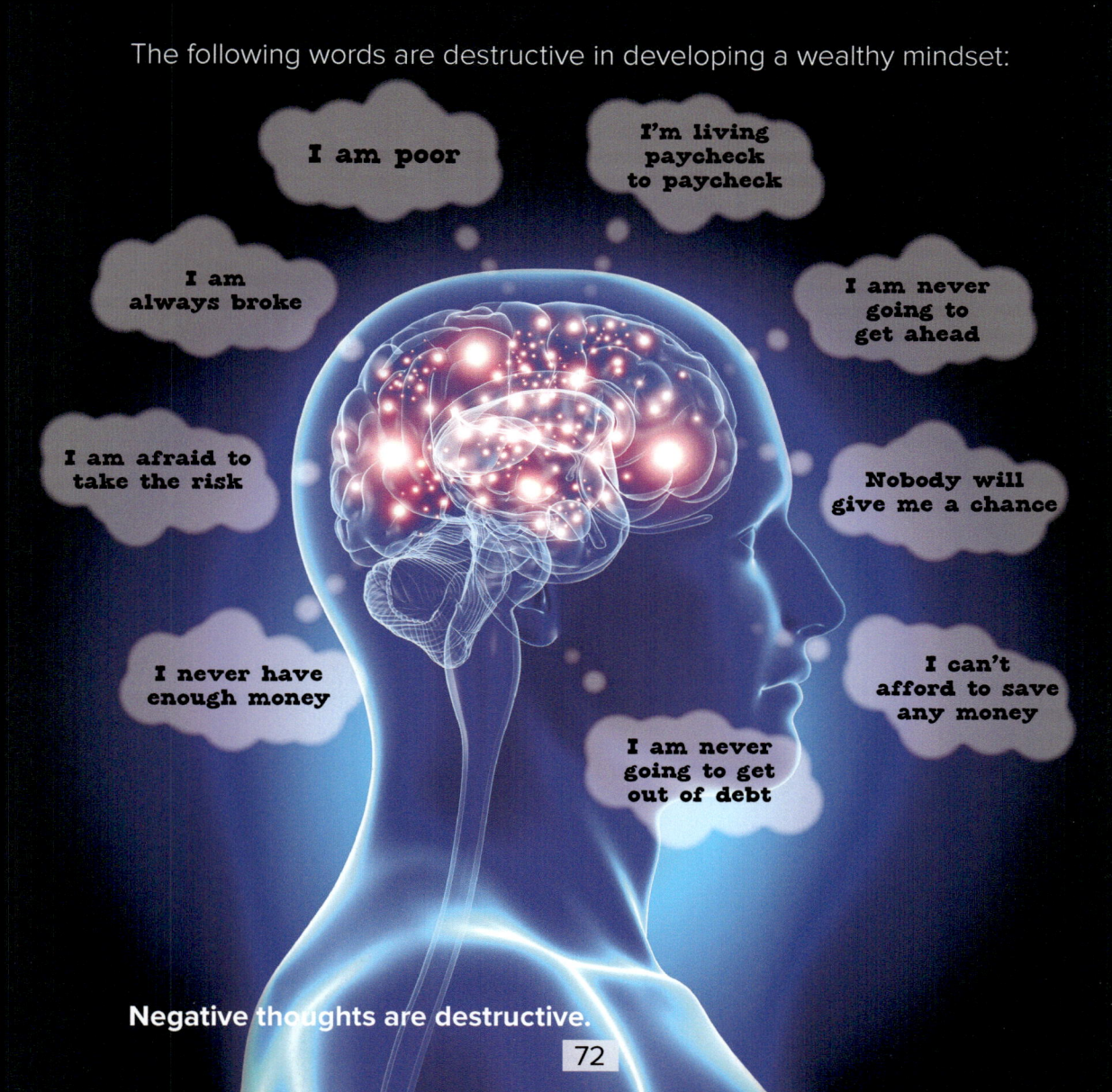

The following words are destructive in developing a wealthy mindset:

- I am poor
- I'm living paycheck to paycheck
- I am always broke
- I am never going to get ahead
- I am afraid to take the risk
- Nobody will give me a chance
- I never have enough money
- I can't afford to save any money
- I am never going to get out of debt

Negative thoughts are destructive.

Now that you have removed the previous words and phrases from your thoughts, replace them with words that will empower your finances such as:

- I give freely to charity
- I am debt free
- I am responsible for my own financial freedom
- I have a consistent savings plan
- I am a wealth builder
- I have a positive cash flow
- I have multiple streams of income
- I have a working budget
- I have a diversified investment portfolio
- I have a sound financial plan that works

Positive thoughts create wealth.

You are the only person who has the power to create wealth in your life. Develop a wealthy mindset and you will be on the road to true wealth.

INSURANCE AND ANNUITY

- Disability Insurance replaces your income in the event of a disabling event.
    Short Term, Long Term

- Long Term Care Insurance is needed when someone with a disability, a long-term physical illness, or a cognitive impairment (such as Alzheimer's disease) can no longer care for himself or herself.

- Life Insurance helps you insure that the goals and dreams of your family, business, loved ones, church, and community will be achieved.
    Whole Life, Universal Life, Variable Life, Term

- Annuity provides you with tax-deferred growth with no maximum contribution limit. It also creates a guaranteed income stream for life.
    Fixed, Indexed, Variable

Life Insurance Options

Permanent Insurance

- **Whole Life:** An insurance product with guaranteed level premiums, death benefit protection and cash value accumulation. The cash value accumulates based on the amount of dividend earned on an annual basis. The dividend scale with an interest component is generally declared on an annual basis.

- **Variable Universal Life:** An insurance product that allows you to vary the frequency and amount of premium payments. It provides a guaranteed minimum death benefit. The cash value accumulates based on the policy premiums that are invested in the investment options available within the insurance company's separate account investment portfolio. This aspect of the cash value is not guaranteed.

However, a fixed account option is available that provides a guarantee.

- **Universal Life:** A flexible insurance product that allows you to modify the policy face amount or premium. A portion of the premium is deposited in the insurance company's conservative investment portfolio, where it earns a specified rate of return and builds cash value. The rate of return earned is generally comparable to the type of rate earned in a Fixed Annuity or CD.

Temporary Insurance

- **Term Life:** Guaranteed death benefit for a specified period of time. There is no cash value accumulation within the plan. Once the term expires, the life insurance coverage disappears. The terms are usually annual renewable, 5 years, 10 years, or 20 years. Term insurance is convertible to permanent insurance. It is the least expensive form of life insurance.

Long Term Care Insurance

Are you and or someone you love age 50 or older? Does your gene pool predict longevity in your future? If so, consider Long Term Care Insurance.

Long Term Care Insurance is designed to cover the costs of skilled nursing care and personal care in a nursing home facility, assisted living facility, adult day care center, or your home. It covers services that pertain to assisting you in your activities of daily living; bathing, eating, dressing, toileting, continence, and transferring.

Fact: Medicare does not pay for long term care needs. As well, your standard health insurance policy does not cover long term care needs.

It is estimated that 9 million Americans needed long term care services in 2005. By 2020, the number is expected to increase to 12 million.

Today, the average costs of long term care coverage in the United States is $81,000

Footnote: Long Term Care Insurance is not just for the elderly. Anyone can apply as long as you are in good health.

Long Term Care Data

2012 National Median Average Service Provider Costs

Homemaker Services (Licensed):
$18.00 per hour

Home Health Aide:
$19.00 per hour

Adult Day Care:
$61.00 per day

Assisted Living Facility (One Bedroom ‚Äì Single occupancy): **$3300.00 per month**

Nursing Home Semi-Private Room (Skilled Nursing Unit): **$200.00 per day**

Nursing Home Private Room (Skilled Nursing Unit): **$222.00 per day**

Source: Genworth Cost of Care 2012 Study

Annuity Options

- Fixed: An annuity with a guaranteed rate of interest for a specified period of time. (No market risk.)

- Equity Indexed: An annuity which combines the stability and tax deferral of a traditional fixed annuity with interest rates linked to a U.S. Stock and or Bond Market Index. (S&P 500 Index, Dow Jones Index, Lehman Treasury Index, etc.) [Minimum guaranteed interest rate provided.]

- Variable: An annuity which provides you with the advantage of tax deferred growth while investing through various mutual fund like investment options. [Risk of loss due to market volatility.]

Seek advice from a trusted licensed financial professional before making insurance choices.

AND THE QUESTION IS...
DO YOU HAVE INSURANCE?

Have you ever considered what your life would be like if you did not have a sound insurance plan? Hypothetically, let's review the roles that insurance plays in your day to day life.

Life Event 1

During your annual check up you are diagnosed with an illness that requires immediate surgery. You check in the hospital and they ask you, **"do you have insurance?"** With insurance, your cost of the treatment will be $1000 copay or deductible. Without the insurance, your treatment will cost $75,000 out of pocket.

Without a good health insurance plan, your financial assets can be wiped out.

Life Event 2
In the midst of your child's birthday party, a lighted match drops on the curtain setting it ablaze and your entire family room goes up in flames. The first question that you are asked, **"do you have insurance?"** With insurance, your cost to restore your home is the $500 deductible. Without insurance, your cost to restore your home is $50,000.

An adequate property & casualty plan makes a difference in your family's safety in the event of an emergency.

Life Event 3
After a successful surgery, your recuperation period will be six to nine months. You contact your creditors to inform them that you are currently not earning an income due to disability. Your creditors ask you, **"do you have insurance?"** With insurance, you will receive a replacement income while you are disabled that enables you to uphold your financial responsibilities. Without insurance, you will have no income, risking your ability to survive.

Disability insurance will afford you the comfort to recuperate with peace of mind.

Life Event 4

You are a single parent with two teenage children. You have a $200,000 mortgage and you hope to send your children to college. You pass away suddenly in a tragic car accident. Your family is asked the question; "do you have insurance?" With insurance, your services will be paid, your children will be able to go to college and keep the family home.

A solid life insurance plan will provide your loved ones with the resources to live out your family's goals.

The recurring question in each situation is, **"Do you have insurance?"** In other words, "Show Me the Money!" When people do business with you, they want to know that they will be paid. Insurance is another form of money. Without insurance (money) your financial stability will suffer a huge blow when faced with life's uncertainties.

Do you have insurance?

LIFE INSURANCE CALCULATOR

The Life Insurance Calculator helps you determine the amount of coverage you need.

Liquidable Assets	Monetary Value	Cash Needs and Installment Debts	Amount Needed
Savings/Checking	$ _____	Immediate Cash Account	$ _____
Certificate of Deposit	_____	(Burial expenses, medical expenses, court costs, etc.)	
Money Market Acc.	_____		
Retirement Accounts	_____	Mortgage, Rent Payment Account	$ _____
Stock	_____	(Mortgage balances or monthly rent * 120 months)	
Mutual Funds	_____		
Other	_____	Child Care Account	$ _____
Subtotal Liquid Assets	_____	(Living expenses, nanny, day care, wedding)	

Current Life Insurance

Company	Death Benefit
_____	$ _____
_____	_____
_____	_____

Installment Debt Account $ _____
(Installment credit, unpaid loans outstanding bills)

Education Account $ _____
(College tuition, vocational school)

Subtotal Life Insurance

$ _____

Emergency Account $ _____
(Unbudgeted expenses=40% of income)

Total Cash Needs and Installment Debt $ _____
Minus
Total assets & Present Life Insurance $ _____

Total Life Insurance Needed $ _____

Types of Wealth Building Plans

- Individual Retirement Account (IRA)
- 403b
- 401k
- Investment Portfolio
  – Stocks, Bonds, Mutual Funds, etc.
- 529 Plan
- Life Insurance Cash Values
- Real Estate Investments
- Business Ownership

Seek advice from a trusted licensed Financial professional before making investments.

Stock = Equity Security

- **Buying ownership in a specific company or corporation. The level of risk varies based on the specific company in which you are investing. Though, it is important not to weight the majority of your money in individual stock from one company.**
  Large Cap, Mid Cap, Small Cap, Growth, Value, International, Global, Sector

Stock = Equity Security
Buying ownership in a specific company or corporation. The level of risk varies based on the specific company in which you are investing. Though, it is important not to weight the majority of your money in individual stock from one company.
Large Cap, Mid Cap, Small Cap, Growth, Value, International, Global, Sector

Bond = Debt Security
Loaning your money to a specific company, corporation or municipality. Generally, the level of risk associated with bonds is low compared to stock. A set annual interest rate is assigned to the bond for a specific period of time. The risk is associated with the (lendee) company's ability to repay your money at maturity.
Corporate, Government, Municipal

Mutual Fund
Investing in a portfolio of stocks and or bonds. The level of risk varies from low to high depending on the portfolio mix. A mutual fund is the "wisest" investment when investing in the market for future growth. The law requires that no more than 5% of one corporation's stock/bond be held in any given fund. This creates a greater amount of diversification because if one corporation collapses the effect on your investment will not be as great as if you separately owned the individual stock or bond.

INVESTMENT

TYPES OF MUTUAL FUNDS

Stock Fund: Invest in stocks only.

Moderate to Aggressive risk.

Large Stocks: Average Annual Return 1926-2018 = 10.0%
Small Stocks: Average Annual Return 1926-2018 = 11.8%
(Source: Ibbotson SBBI)

Types of Stock Funds: Growth Fund, Growth & Income Fund, Value Fund, International Stock Fund, Global Stock Fund, Large Cap Stock Fund, Mid Cap Stock Fund, Small Cap Stock Fund, Sector Fund, Index Fund

Bond Fund: Invest in bonds only.

Low to Moderately Aggressive risk.

Corporate Bonds: Average Annual Return 1926-2018 = 5.6%
Long Term Government Bonds: Average Annual Return 1926-2018 = 5.5%
Treasury Bills: Average Annual Return 1926-2018 = 3.3%
(Source: Ibbotson SBBI/Vanguard)

Types of Bond Funds: Corporate Bond Fund, U.S. Gov't Bond Fund, International Bond Fund, Global Bond Fund, Municipal Bond Fund (Structured for tax free growth. However, consult with your tax advisor.)

Balanced Fund: Invest in a balance of stocks and bonds.

Moderate risk.

Average Annual Return 1926-2018 = 7.8%
(Source: Vanguard)

Inflation: Average Annual Return: 1926 - 2018 = 2.9%

Past performance is no guarantee of future results.

WEALTH BUILDING EXERCISES

Create a Family Financial Time - Evaluate your "Wealth Builders Blueprint" quarterly, semi-annually or at least once per year. If there are children within the household, include them in the family financial discussion.

A child exposed to wealth building principles is better equipped to become a wealthy adult.

Reevaluate these financial tools during your family financial time:

- Cash Flow Calculator
- Budget Planner
- Net Worth Calculator

These tools will help you stay on target as you build your wealth.

88

WEALTH IS RELATIVE

As you come to the conclusion of The Road to Wealth Begins with You, Volume Two of The Financial Truth™ book series, understand that wealth is relative.

You might come from a family that has passed a mindset of "poverty" from generation to generation. If you have continuously lived life paycheck to paycheck, wealth to you can be breaking the vicious cycle of poverty and learning to live below your means. To a parent, wealth can be health, safety and a financially secure future for their children. To a professional athlete or an entrepreneur, the monetary level of success they have achieved often measures wealth. And to the philanthropist, wealth is having so much; they can give it away.

Don't allow society to make you believe that wealth is only about being a multimillionaire or billionaire.

Wealth is leaving your future generations better off than you are, i.e., financially, spiritually, relationally, etc. Whatever way you measure wealth, understand this, "wealth must manifest itself within your mind, before it can exist in the tangible".

Commit to living a life that manifests wealth within your being. Learn to live with a wealthy mindset.

WEALTH EMPOWERMENT OATH

Recite the Wealth Empowerment Oath daily, and wealth will dwell within your life.

Money, I, (state your name), am not intimidated by you any more. I am in control of you. You will not control me. Money, I am no longer allowing you to cause pain in my life. Money, if I don't have enough of you, I will learn how to manage with what I have. However, I am effectively utilizing wise money management strategies to improve and empower my financial worth. I am living with a "wealthy state of mind".

My money helps me, not hinders me. My money empowers me, not cripples me. Any financial curse that has been placed on my life is now broken. I am not allowing my debt to hold me hostage any longer now that I have a "wealthy state of mind". I am freeing myself of "bad" debt and irresponsible financial decisions. I am paying myself, before I pay anyone else. I am saving first and spending second.

I, (state your name), am obtaining my wealth through acquiring appreciable assets, not depreciable assets. I am obtaining my wealth through an accumulation plan, not a consumption plan. I am patient and disciplined as my net worth grows and grows and grows. I am focused and maintaining a positive state of mind. I am unselfish with my money though I will make wise decisions on whom I will share my money with. I am living with a "wealthy state of mind".

Money is my tool. And with my tool I am building a strong financial foundation that is empowering my family and me henceforth and forever more.

I am living with a "WEALTHY STATE OF MIND".

"The Road to Wealth Begins with You™" has been created to help you develop a positive, healthy, and spiritual relationship with your money.

Money does not have the power to do or be anything until you attach your spirit to it. It can't make you wealthy or poor, for these are just states of mind. Approach your money with the understanding that it is a tool to help you empower your life and the lives of those around you.

Understand that your ability to live according to the Wealth Builders Blueprint plays a key role in your financial success. Exercise wisdom in your life's choices. Don't allow the financial mistakes in your past to destroy your ability to build wealth. Utilize the budget planner, cash flow calculator, expense tracker, and other financial tools to help you stay on course on your wealth journey. Apply the principles that you were taught concerning stability and growth to secure and build your wealth. Exercise patience.

Remain true to your commitment to build a concrete financial foundation that will empower you as you achieve your financial goals. Remember that your knowledge must continue to be nurtured to end the cycle of financial destruction, and pass on "The Financial Truth™" to future generations.

The Road to Wealth Begins with You!

BIO

Carla a Financial Professional, Author and Inspirational Speaker, has committed her life to economically and financially empower the community. She attributes her commitment and passion to her relationship with God and fulfilling her divine purpose.

Carla is a graduate of Hampton University in Hampton, VA. She has been a practicing Financial Professional since 1992. She is the Founder / CEO of Genesis One Wealth Builders, Sugar Land, TX.

As an Advocate for Economic and Financial Empowerment for the community, Carla is a frequently featured television and radio guest throughout the United States. As well, she has been a featured Financial Advisor for major television networks in the Houston area. Carla is a sought-out speaker on the topics of "Wealth and Abundance", "God and Money", and "Financial and Economic Empowerment" across America.

Carla is the author of "The Financial Truth" book series and the National Urban League's nationally acclaimed Economic Empowerment program entitled, "Know Your Money".

Programs written and taught by Carla have impacted over One Million Americans since the year 2002.

Carla hosted the internationally acclaimed Internet talk radio show; "The Financial Truth with Carla Cargle" on the Voice America network reaching listeners around the world. Carla has interviewed some of the world's greatest voices on wealth; John Randolph Price, Dr. John F. DeMartini, and many others.

She is a resident of the Houston, Texas metropolitan area.

GLOSSARY OF TERMS
Source Investopedia Dictionary

401(k): A tax-deferred contribution plan set up by an employer that allows employees to deduct a portion of their salary from their paycheck to be set aside for retirement on a pre-tax basis. Maximum contribution limits do apply. If you withdraw money from the plan before age 59 1/2 , a 10% withdrawal penalty will apply. (Exceptions may apply for the 10% penalty. Seek help from a licensed financial professional.)

403(b): A tax deferred retirement plan that is the equivalent of a 401(k) plan but for qualifying non-profit organizations, public schools, and municipal agencies.

529 Plan: A savings plan designed to give tax-free advantages to encourage savings for future higher education costs.

Appreciable Asset: Asset that increases in value.

Asset: A resource than an individual, corporation, or country owns or controls that has economic value and that is expected to provide future benefit. A balance sheet item representing what someone owns.

Commodity: An agricultural product (soybeans, grains, coffee, etc.), a metal, financial indices, wood or any other physical substance that investors buy or sell.

Depreciable Asset: Asset that decreases in value.

Dividend: Distribution of a portion of the company's earnings.

Dollar Cost Averaging: The technique of buying a fixed dollar amount of a particular investment on a regular schedule, regardless of the share price. More shares are purchased when the price is low, less shares are purchased when the price is high.

Dow Jones Industrial Average: A weighted list of 30 frequently traded Blue Chip company stocks on the New York Stock Exchange or the NASDAQ.

Estate: An individual's valuables. i.e. Investments, Real Estate, Life Insurance, Fine Art, etc.

Executor/Executrix: A person designated in a decedent's will to carry out the directions and requests in the will and to dispose of the property according to the testamentary provisions. (Executor is a male. Executrix is a female.)

Global Fund: The fund invests in companies within the United States and overseas.

Growth Fund: A diversified portfolio of stocks that has capital appreciation (growth in price) as its primary goal, and invests in companies that reinvest their earnings into expansion, research and development, and acquisitions.

Income Fund: A fund, which seeks to provide a stable, current income by investing in securities that pay interest and or dividends.

Index Fund: A portfolio of investments that are weighted the same as a stock exchange index in order to mirror its performance. (Stock Exchange Index: Dow Jones Industrial Average, S&P 500 Index, Treasury Index, etc.)

International Fund: The fund invests in companies outside of the United States.

IRA (Individual Retirement Account): A self directed, tax deferred retirement account established by an employed worker who earns a wage, salary, or self-employment income. Annual maximum contribution limits do apply. Deposits into a Traditional IRA are tax deductible. (Restrictions do apply) Deposits into a Roth IRA are not tax deductible, but the money grows tax-free.

Large Cap Fund: A fund that invests in companies valued between $10 billion and $200 billion.

Liability: A debt or outstanding obligation.

Mid Cap Fund: A fund that invests in companies valued between $2 billion and $10 billion.

NASDAQ: The first electronic stock market. It is traditionally home to high-tech stocks. It handles computerized trading for over 5,000 over-the-counter stocks.

New York Stock Exchange: A corporation responsible for listing securities, setting policies, and supervising the buying and selling of securities. Floor traders (people) make the trades.

Net Worth: The amount by which your assets exceed your liabilities. (Deduct what you owe from what you own.) Sector Fund: The fund invests in companies within a specific industry. Ex. Health Care Fund, Technology Fund, etc. Securities: Stocks, Bonds, Mutual Funds, etc.

Small Cap Fund: A fund that invests in companies valued between $300 million and $2 billion.

S&P 500 Index (Standard & Poor's): A weighted list of 500 frequently traded Large Cap company stocks on the New York Stock Exchange.

Treasury Index: An index that is used to determine interest rate changes for certain adjustable rate mortgages.

Trust: A legal contract between the grantor (creator) and the trustee, which gives ownership to a trustee to manage wealth and direct income for the benefit of another.

Trustee: An individual who holds or manages assets for the benefit of another.

Value Fund: A fund that primarily holds stocks that are deemed to be undervalued in price.

Will: A legal document that directs the transferal of an individuals assets at death.

APPENDIX

Resources for statistical information:

U.S. Census 2010
U.S. Payment Card Information Network
Adm. Office U.S. Courts Bankruptcy Filings
Federal Reserve
www.medicare.gov

Recommended Publications and Resources:

The Dynamic Laws of Prosperity, Author: Catherine Ponder
The Little Money Bible, Author: Stuart Wilde
The Abundance Book, Author: John Randolph Price

WHAT'S IT WORTH?

Is it an appreciable (A) or depreciable asset (D)? What do you own?

Coach Bag	D
Michael Jordan Baseball Card	A
CLK Mercedes Benz 2005	D
Real Estate	A
Gucci Suit	D
Apple Stock	A
A pair of Jimmy Choo Shoes	D
Diamond Jewelry	A
Neiman Marcus Gift Card	D
Retirement Account	A
Xbox	D
529 Plan	A

Answer key for page 67

Wealth Builders Money Personality Scoring Guide

SD = Strongly disagree
D = Disagree
N = Neutral
A = Agree
SA = Strongly Agree

MM = Mattress Mogul
B&B = Broke & Beggin'
SP = Sales Pro
LL = Living Large
Bal = Balanced

Instructions: Circle your response for each question. Add up the number of responses per money personality and write the number on the line corresponding with each money personality. Add up the Wealth Builder's responses and the Wealth Destroyer's responses. Whichever area you scored the highest identifies your money personality.

Example 1: (12 questions per section)			
Wealth Builder		Wealth Destroyer	
Mattress Mogul	2	Sales Pro	1
Balanced	7	B&B	0
		Livin' Large	2
Total Score	9	Total Score	3

Based on your score, you are a Balanced/Wealth Builder

Example 2: (12 questions per section)			
Wealth Builder		Wealth Destroyer	
Mattress Mogul	2	Sales Pro	1
Balanced	1	B&B	1
		Livin' Large	7
Total Score	3	Total Score	9

Based on your score, you are a Livin' Large/Wealth Destroyer

Spending Habits

1. SD (SP)　　D (LL)　　N (BB)　　A (MM)　　SA (Bal)
2. SD (Bal)　　D (MM)　　N (BB)　　A (LL)　　SA (SP)
3. SD (Bal)　　D (MM)　　N (BB)　　A (SP)　　SA (LL)
4. SD (Bal)　　D (MM)　　N (BB)　　A (SP)　　SA (LL)
5. SD (Bal)　　D (MM)　　N (SP)　　A (LL)　　SA (BB)
6. SD (BB)　　D (LL)　　N (SP)　　A (Bal)　　SA (MM)
7. SD (LL)　　D (SP)　　N (Bal)　　A (BB)　　SA (MM)
8. SD (Bal)　　D (LL)　　N (SP)　　A (BB)　　SA (MM)
9. SD (MM)　　D (Bal)　　N (BB)　　A (LL)　　SA (SP)
10. SD (Bal)　　D (MM)　　N (SP)　　A (LL)　　SA (BB)
11. SD (Bal)　　D (SP)　　N (BB)　　A (LL)　　SA (MM)
12. SD (MM)　　D (Bal)　　N (SP)　　A (BB)　　SA (LL)

Wealth Builder		Wealth Destroyer	
Mattress Mogul		Sales Pro	
Balanced		B&B	
		Livin' Large	
Total Score		Total Score	

Based on your score, you are a _____ / _____

Wealth Characteristics

1. SD (Bal)   D (MM)   N (BB)   A (SP)   SA (LL)
2. SD (MM)   D (Bal)   N (BB)   A (SP)   SA (LL)
3. SD (MM)   D (Bal)   N (SP)   A (BB)   SA (LL)
4. SD (Bal)   D (MM)   N (SP)   A (LL)   SA (BB)
5. SD (LL)   D (BB)   N (SP)   A (MM)   SA (Bal)
6. SD (MM)   D (Bal)   N (SP)   A (LL)   SA (BB)
7. SD (Bal)   D (MM)   N (LL)   A (SP)   SA (BB)
8. SD (Bal)   D (LL)   N (SP)   A (BB)   SA (MM)
9. SD (MM)   D (BB)   N (Bal)   A (SP)   SA (LL)
10. SD (SP)   D (MM)   N (BB)   A (LL)   SA (Bal)
11. SD (Bal)   D (LL)   N (BB)   A (MM)   SA (SP)
12. SD (MM)   D (LL)   N (BB)   A (SP)   SA (Bal)

Wealth Builder		Wealth Destroyer	
Mattress Mogul		Sales Pro	
Balanced		B&B	
		Livin' Large	
Total Score		Total Score	

Based on your score, you are a _____ / _____

Financial Stability

1. SD (BB)   D (MM)   N (LL)   A (SP)   SA (Bal)
2. SD Bal)   D (MM)   N (BB)   A (SP)   SA (LL)
3. SD (Bal)   D (MM)   N (SP)   A (LL)   SA (BB)
4. SD (MM)   D (Bal)   N (BB)   A (SP)   SA (LL)
5. SD (BB)   D (SP)   N (LL)   A (MM)   SA (Bal)
6. SD (BB)   D (LL)   N (SP)   A (MM)   SA (Bal)
7. SD (Bal)   D (MM)   N (LL)   A (SP)   SA (BB)
8. SD (BB)   D (LL)   N (SP)   A (MM)   SA (Bal)
9. SD (Bal)   D (MM)   N (BB)   A (SP)   SA (LL)
10. SD (BB)   D (SP)   N (MM)   A (LL)   SA (Bal)
11. SD (BB)   D (SP)   N (LL)   A (MM)   SA (Bal)
12. SD (BB)   D (LL)   N (SP)   A (MM)   SA (Bal)

Wealth Builder		Wealth Destroyer	
Mattress Mogul		Sales Pro	
Balanced		B&B	
		Livin' Large	
Total Score		Total Score	

Based on your score, you are a _____ / _____

To request Carla to speak or facilitate a workshop send an email request to: Carla@carlacargle.com

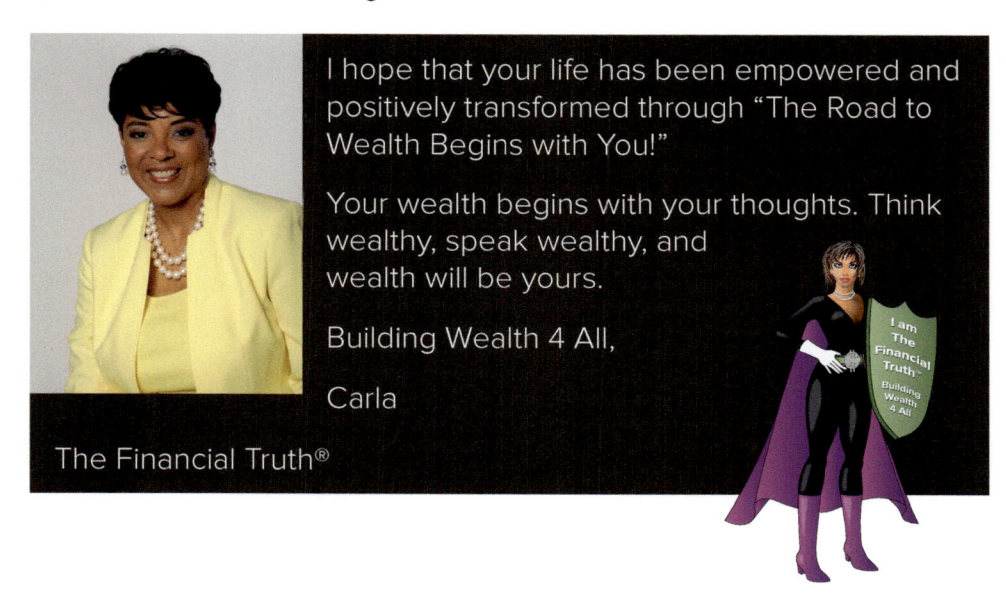

I hope that your life has been empowered and positively transformed through "The Road to Wealth Begins with You!"

Your wealth begins with your thoughts. Think wealthy, speak wealthy, and wealth will be yours.

Building Wealth 4 All,

Carla

The Financial Truth®

To become a part of The Financial Truth Community Log into www.carlacargle.com and join our mailing list.

To purchase The Financial Truth book series; please visit Wealth Builders Publishing House www.wbphbooks.com.

The Financial Truth book series:
Wealth Journal
Volume One - Your Mind, Your Mouth, and Your Money.
Volume Two - The Road to Wealth begins with You.
Volume Three - Humble, Wise and Wealthy Living.

Humble, Wise, and Wealthy Living.

"Humble, Wise and Wealthy Living"

By: Carla J. Cargle WBPH
Wealth Empowerment book written from a spiritual perspective.

The Financial Truth™
I am The Financial Truth™
Building Wealth 4 All